30 Degrees on Bypass

Dr. A. H. Yurvati

Yurvati Legacy Press
www.yurvatibooks.com
info@yurvatibooks.com

Table of Contents

To my lovely wife, Sharon. Without her guidance, encouragement, and love, I would not have had such a successful career. To my friends, colleagues, residents, and students whom I have had the pleasure of growing up with, working with or teaching. If you identify yourself in my book, it's because you intersected with me in a special way. Finally, to all of my patients who entrusted me to care for them at their most vulnerable time—I saved many, some I could not—I always gave my best.

Chapter 1

I hope you liked my first two books: *Wet My Hands* and *This to Me*. I was able to transfer royalties to the TCOM and University of Strathclyde general scholarship fund, so I thank you for your purchases. Book three, *30 Degrees on Bypass,* will be a continuation of my life's journey with the Fates. I will revisit sections I presented in book one and two in more depth. Let's proceed and see if the Fates are continuing to interfere with my life.

Chapter 2

Just when I thought the Fates were busy with other activities, they came back. I was having severe left shoulder pain I thought it was a rotator cuff. I consulted an orthopedic joint specialist, and sure enough, significant joint degeneration, bone on bone, not a rotator cuff. Dr. Andrew recommended a total shoulder replacement. The cause was the high dose steroids I was receiving with my chemotherapy. Dexamethasone is a corticosteroid commonly used in humans and domestic animals, particularly in the treatment of painful conditions. When articular cartilage cells were subjected to dexamethasone, cell proliferation was inhibited. Even more significant than that was the fact that dexamethasone induced cell apoptosis. Apoptosis is a form of programmed cell death. In simple terms, dexamethasone caused chondrocytes to die a premature death. The mechanism by which corticosteroids does this is most likely through blocking the anti-apoptotic effects of Insulin-like growth factor (IGF-1).

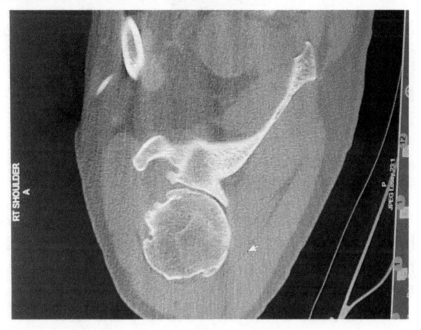

I underwent a total shoulder replacement. The scalene block lasted forty-eight hours, so no real post-operative pain. The only issue was wearing a sling and no driving for two weeks. Fortunately, Lara came down from Washington to help us for two weeks; she was an angel. I did have a post-operative complication not related to the shoulder replacement. I went into acute right ventricular failure, got admitted, and diuresis removed 15 pounds of water weight!

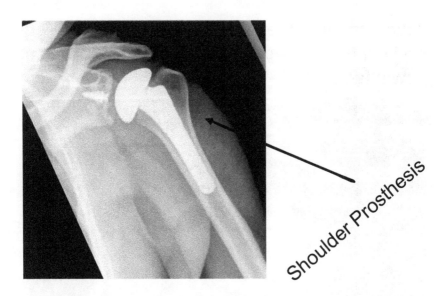

Shoulder Prosthesis

Well, the Fates got this one, but my recovery has been great. I was driving and had an increased range of motion. Unfortunately, we need to evaluate the right shoulder.

I overused during my recovery and now have the same symptoms. So, I will undergo right shoulder replacement in April. All went well with the second implant. That was until the Fates got involved. I was having severe pain in both rotator cuffs while floating in the pool with a noodle. My initial thought was capsulitis, but it was bilateral rotator cuff tears.

That meant removal with conversion to a total implant. The right side was completed on October 2023. The left side underwent a redo on February 2024.

The Fates got me again; the left shoulder prosthesis is loose, and he wants to do a third revision! Not sure if the end result will be an increase in range of motion.

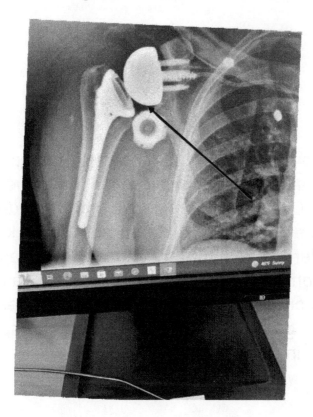

Chapter 3

The Fates keep taunting me! I developed a raging septic phlebitis of my right hand the week before Christmas. I got septic and was admitted on three IV antibiotics in early septic shock. I had to undergo hand surgery to drain the phlegmon. A phlegmon is different than an abscess, as there is no contained wall. A phlegmon just destroys tissue. I got immediate relief and was completely healed in three weeks.

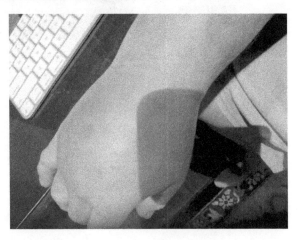

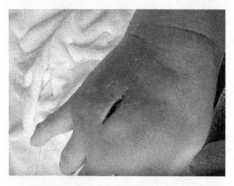

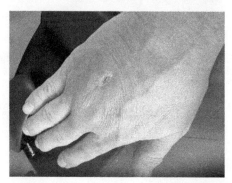

Completely healed, I now have my first stigmata—I guess all of that Catholic upbringing is coming to pass.

You're not going to believe this, but I developed the same on my left hand. I now have two stigmata.

Stigmata

Chapter 4

Grade School

Many Catholic parishes had grade schools associated with the home church. I believe it was a way to indoctrinate Catholicism. We were enrolled in Sacred Heart School, which was built in 1905.

Sacred Heart School

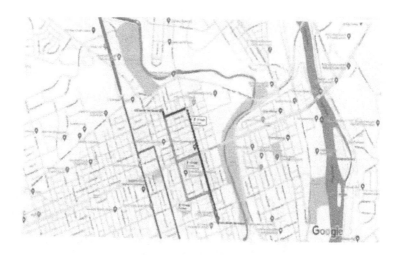

We walked from 922 North Fifth Street to 325 N Fourth Street every school day rain, shine, or snow; the distance was 1.7 miles each way. We did not have buses or carpool.

A high school classmate, Jim, was the principal of Sacred Heart; he was up in the attic and found a box with report cards. He contacted me and asked if I wanted copies. Much to my surprise, he sent me the originals signed by the nuns to include two of the Fates!

Grade1 Transfer from Washington (public school) to Sacred Heart

LAST NAME	FIRST NAME AND INITIALS
Yurwati	Albert A.

PUPIL'S REPORT FOR YEAR ENDING JUNE 30, 1962

NUMBER OF SESSIONS	PERIOD 1	2	3	TERM TOTAL	PERIOD 1	2	3	TERM TOTAL
PRESENT				140	50	65	58	173
ABSENT				0	8	5	7	17
LATE				0	0	0	0	0

TRAITS	7 WKS.	13 WKS.	1st TERM	7 WKS.	13 WKS.	2nd TERM
COOPERATION			B'	B'	B'	B
SELF-CONTROL			B	B'	B	B
PERSEVERANCE			B	B	B	B
COURAGE			B	B	B	B
PROMPTNESS			B'	B	B	B
ORDERLINESS			B	B	B	B
HEALTH HABITS			B'	B'	B	B

SUBJECTS	7 WKS.	13 WKS.	1st TERM	7 WKS.	13 WKS.	2nd TERM
ENGLISH ORAL			80	80	80	80
ENGLISH WRITTEN						
ENGLISH READING			80	80	80	85
ENGLISH SPELLING				80	75	80
SOCIAL STUDIES HISTORY						
SOCIAL STUDIES GEOGRAPHY						
SOCIAL STUDIES CIVICS						
ARITHMETIC			75	70	70	75
HANDWRITING			80	80	75	80
NATURE STUDY						
ART			80	80	80	80
MUSIC			80	80	80	80
INDUSTRIAL ARTS						
CLOTHING INSTRUCTION			85	85	80	85
PHYSICAL EDUCATION						
HEALTH EDUCATION					80	
GENERAL ESTIMATE						

ITEMS NEEDING SPECIAL ATTENTION	PERIOD 1	2	3	PERIOD 1	2	3
REGULARITY OF ATTENDANCE						
HABITS OF THOROUGHNESS			80	80	80	80
HABITS OF ATTENTION			80	80	85	85
HABITS OF HOME STUDY			80	80	85	85

SUMMARY OF SESSIONS ABSENT

SESSIONS OF ABSENCE	NON-COMP. AGE TERM END. JAN.	COMP. AGE TERM END. JUNE	TOTAL FOR YEAR
EXCUSED	0	17	17
PARENTAL NEGLECT			
ILLEGAL EMPLOYMENT			
TRUANCY			
TOTAL	0	17	17

NUMBER OF SESSIONS
NUMBER OF TIMES REPORTED FOR VERIFICATION

REMARKS:
Admitted October 9, 1961.

ROUTINE MEDICAL EXAMINATION

DATE EXAMINED	PHYSICAL DEFECTS RECOMMENDED FOR TREATMENT	DATE TREATED

C. P1

Grade 2

LAST NAME						FIRST NAME AND INITIALS					
Yurvati						Albert H.					

PUPIL'S REPORT FOR YEAR ENDING JUNE 30, 1968

SUMMARY OF SESSIONS ABSENT

NUMBER OF SESSIONS	PERIOD 1	2	TERM TOTAL	PERIOD 3	4	TERM TOTAL
PRESENT	83	80	168	92	100	192
ABSENT	2	0	0	0	0	0
LATE	0	0	0	0	0	0

TRAITS	FIRST QUARTER	FIRST TERM	THIRD QUARTER	SECOND TERM
COOPERATION	B	B	B	A
SELF-CONTROL	B	B	B	A
PERSEVERANCE	B	B	A	A
COURAGE	B	B	B	A
PROMPTNESS	B	B	A	A
ORDERLINESS	B	B	B	A
HEALTH HABITS	B	B	B	A

SUBJECTS		FIRST QUARTER	FIRST TERM	THIRD QUARTER	SECOND TERM
ENGLISH	ORAL	86	88	91	92
	WRITTEN	86	89	96	92
	READING	78	81	96	90
	SPELLING	86	86	95	94
SOCIAL STUDIES	HISTORY	72	76	86	88
	GEOGRAPHY	90	92	92	89
	CIVICS				
ARITHMETIC		77	80	87	87
SCIENCE		75	80	86	90
HANDWRITING		78	79	85	90
ART		80	80	86	86
MUSIC		82	80	85	90
Religion		85	88	96	90
PHYSICAL EDUCATION					
HEALTH EDUCATION		72	75	86	85
GENERAL AVERAGE					

SESSIONS OF ABSENCE	NON-COMP. TERM END. JAN. JUNE	COMP. AGE TERM END. JAN. JUNE	TOTAL FOR YEAR
EXCUSED			0 0 0
PARENTAL NEGLECT			
ILLEGAL EMPLOYMENT			
TRUANCY			
TOTAL			0 0 0

NUMBER OF SESSIONS
NUMBER OF TIMES REPORTED FOR VERIFICATION

REMARKS: 105 - 62 - 6 - 61 - 6

TEACHER'S SIGNATURE

Sr. M. St. Raymund

ITEMS NEEDING SPECIAL ATTENTION	PERIOD 1	2	PERIOD 3	4
HABITS OF THOROUGHNESS	90	91	90	90
HABITS OF ATTENTION	70	90	96	90
HABITS OF HOME STUDY	85	85	96	91
READING LEVEL—G. E.	7.4	8.0		

TESTING PROGRAM

DATE	NAME OF TEST	FORM	RESULTS
9/26/67	Cath. Messenger		Voc 8.4 Read 6.8
11/67			7.4
10/68	Catholic Messenger		Nov 8.6 Read 8.3
2-1-68	Otis Lennon Ability	G	105 - 62 - 6 - 61 - 6

Grade 3

LAST NAME: Yurvati,

FIRST NAME AND INITIALS: Albert H.

PUPIL'S REPORT FOR YEAR ENDING JUNE 30, 1967

NUMBER OF SESSIONS	PERIOD 1	2	TERM TOTAL	PERIOD 3	4	TERM TOTAL
PRESENT	92	1/2	174	88	98	186
ABSENT						
LATE						

TRAITS	FIRST QUARTER	FIRST TERM	THIRD QUARTER	SECOND TERM
COOPERATION	B+	a	a	a
SELF-CONTROL	B	a	a	a
PERSEVERANCE	B	a	a	a
COURAGE	B	a	a	a
PROMPTNESS	B+	a	a	a
ORDERLINESS	B+	a	a	a
HEALTH HABITS	B+	a	a	a

SUBJECTS		FIRST QUARTER	FIRST TERM	THIRD QUARTER	SECOND TERM
ENGLISH	ORAL	85	86	88	89
	WRITTEN	85	90	90	86
	READING	90	90	92	90
	SPELLING	90	88	90	90
SOCIAL STUDIES	HISTORY	85	92	91	92
	GEOGRAPHY	85	90	91	93
	CIVICS				
ARITHMETIC		82	86	88	87
SCIENCE		87	90	94	95
HANDWRITING		75	80	80	82
ART		75	80	80	82
MUSIC		80	85	85	85
Religion		87	90	90	91
PHYSICAL EDUCATION					
HEALTH EDUCATION		85	87	90	90
GENERAL AVERAGE					

ITEMS NEEDING SPECIAL ATTENTION	PERIOD 1	2	PERIOD 3	4
HABITS OF THOROUGHNESS	90	90	90	91
HABITS OF ATTENTION	90	90	96	93
HABITS OF HOME STUDY	80	90	90	93
READING LEVEL—G.E.	7.4		7.8	

SUMMARY OF SESSIONS ABSENT

SESSIONS OF ABSENCE	NON-COMP. TERM END. JAN	JUNE	COMP AGE TERM END. JAN	JUNE	TOTAL FOR YEAR
EXCUSED					
PARENTAL NEGLECT					
ILLEGAL EMPLOYMENT					
TRUANCY					
TOTAL					

TEACHER'S SIGNATURE: St. Constantia

TESTING PROGRAM

DATE	NAME OF TEST	FORM	Voc. Read	RESULTS	G.E.
12-18-66			6.0	9.1	7.4
12-1-66			7.5	7.3	
1-20-67			7.8	7.1	7.4
5-8-67					

Grade 4: One of the Fates!

Grade 5: One of the Fates!

Grade 6

Grade 7

LAST NAME						FIRST NAME AND INITIALS		
Yurvati, Albert H.								

PUPIL'S REPORT FOR YEAR ENDING JUNE 30, 1943

NUMBER OF SESSIONS	PERIOD 1	2	3	TERM TOTAL	PERIOD 1	2	3	TERM TOTAL
PRESENT	57	41	56	160	43	61	60	164
ABSENT	3	1	3	4	15	8	0	23
LATE	0	0	0	0	0	0	0	0

TRAITS	7 WKS.	13 WKS.	1ST TERM	7 WKS.	13 WKS.	2ND TERM
COOPERATION	B	B	B	B	B+	B+
SELF-CONTROL	a	a	a	B	a	a
PERSEVERANCE	a	a	a-	B	B+	a
COURAGE	a	a	a-	a	a	a
PROMPTNESS	B	B+	B	B	a	a
ORDERLINESS	B-	B-	B	B	B	a
HEALTH HABITS	a	a	a-	a	a	a

SUBJECTS		7 WKS.	13 WKS.	1ST TERM	7 WKS.	13 WKS.	2ND TERM
ENGLISH	ORAL	80	80	80	85	85	85
	WRITTEN						
	READING	80	80	85	85	85	85
	SPELLING	80	80	85	80	80	85
SOCIAL STUDIES	HISTORY						
	GEOGRAPHY						
	CIVICS						
ARITHMETIC		75	70	70	65	75	75
HANDWRITING		75	75	80	40	80	80
SCIENCE NATURE STUDY		70	75	70	70	75	80
ART		70	75	75	80	80	80
MUSIC		70	75	75	75	80	80
INDUSTRIAL ARTS Religion							
SEWING INSTRUCTION		80	80	80	90	85	85
PHYSICAL EDUCATION							
HEALTH EDUCATION			80	85	85	90	
GENERAL ESTIMATE							

ITEMS NEEDING SPECIAL ATTENTION	PERIOD 1	2	3	PERIOD 1	2	3
REGULARITY OF ATTENDANCE						
HABITS OF THOROUGHNESS	75	75	80	80	80	80
HABITS OF ATTENTION	85	85	85	80	85	85
HABITS OF HOME STUDY	80	85	85	85	85	85

SUMMARY OF SESSIONS ABSENT

1—UNEXCUSED ABSENCE APPLIES TO ALL PUPILS

2—UNLAWFUL ABSENCE APPLIES ONLY TO PUPILS OF COMPULSORY SCHOOL AGE. THIS SHOULD BE INTERPRETED AS THE TIME OF ENTRY INTO SCHOOL (A GRADE, NOT KINDERGARTEN) WHICH SHALL BE NOT LATER THAN THE AGE OF EIGHT YEARS, UNTIL THE AGE OF SEVENTEEN YEARS.

3—IF DURING A TERM THE PUPIL IS PROMOTED FROM KINDERGARTEN TO FIRST GRADE OR BECOMES SIX YEARS OF AGE, THE "SESSIONS ABSENT" ARE TO BE DISTRIBUTED UNDER TWO HEADINGS, "COMPULSORY AGE" AND "NON-COMPULSORY AGE."

4—IN SUMMARIZING CAUSES OF ABSENCE THE "VERIFIED REPORT" IS TO BE TAKEN IN PREFERENCE TO THE "TEACHER RECORD." IF NO VERIFIED REPORT HAS BEEN MADE, THE "TEACHER RECORD" IS TO BE TAKEN.

5—THE TERM AND YEAR TOTALS MUST AGREE WITH THE TERM AND YEAR TOTALS ON THE PUPIL'S REPORT.

SESSIONS OF ABSENCE	NON-COMP. TERM END.		COMP. AGE TERM END.		TOTAL FOR YEAR
	JAN.	JUNE	JAN.	JUNE	
EXCUSED	4	23			27
PARENTAL NEGLECT					
ILLEGAL EMPLOYMENT					
TRUANCY					
TOTAL	4	23			27
NUMBER OF SESSIONS					
NUMBER OF TIMES REPORTED FOR VERIFICATION					

REMARKS:

Sr. Maria Angelica

ROUTINE MEDICAL EXAMINATION

DATE EXAMINED	PHYSICAL DEFECTS RECOMMENDED FOR TREATMENT	DATE TREATED	NOTE:
			AT THE END OF THE SCHOOL YEAR ONE OF THE FOLLOWING THREE ENTRIES SHOULD HAVE BEEN MADE.
			1—DATE AND "NONE" IF NO DEFECTS WERE RECOMMENDED BY THE SCHOOL PHYSICIAN FOR TREATMENT.
			2—DATE AND DEFECTS RECOMMENDED FOR TREATMENT, BY SCHOOL PHYSICIAN, AND DATES OF TREATMENTS IF ANY.
			3—"NO EXAMINATION" IF FOR ANY REASON THE EXAMINATION WAS OMITTED.

C 81

17

Grade 8

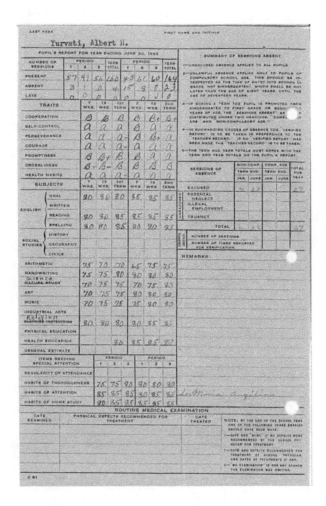

Arithmetic was not my strong point. It goes back to book one describing my time in grade school. I was an overall B+ student—not too bad for lack of studying. I got dinged on handwriting. I guess I was destined to be a doctor! Not sure how they graded habits of thoroughness, habits of attention, habits of home study. I survived grade school then off to high school.

About a month after I received the report cards, the school sustained a massive fire. I believe I have the only original report cards of all of the graduates.

Sacred Heart School Fire

The 115-year-old building has been torn down, and there is tension between the high school and Sacred Heart church as to who owns the land.

Sacred Heart Church

Alter Boy

Chapter 5

High School

Founded in 1926 by the Right Reverend Leo Gregory Fink, Allentown Central Catholic High School (ACCHS) has expanded for its humble beginnings as Masson Memorial School into a major educational complex. The addition of Rockne Hall in 1940 and Barry Hall in 1964 completed this educational facility.

Allentown Central Catholic High School

Mason Hall

Rockne Hall

I did not do well in high school. My father said there was no money for college, so I should join the service. I explored the US Army at the advice of Mr. Ritter, the pharmacist I worked for, and indeed I found training as an advanced medic. The Fates directed me to sign up. Little did I know this was the best direction and influenced my future. We were still at war in Viet Nam, and my draft card number was 3 (!), a sure-fire statistical guarantee of being drafted. Enlisting seemed to be my only option. My ASVAB (Armed Services Vocational Aptitude Battery) scores were excellent "per the recruiter," and I was guaranteed an MOS (Military Occupation Specialty). I chose advanced 91C, Practical Nursing Specialist. The recruiter came to our house and met with my parents, and we signed papers allowing me to enlist. I was going in the Army after graduation.

No money, no grades (academically ranked 203 out of 281) college was not an option.

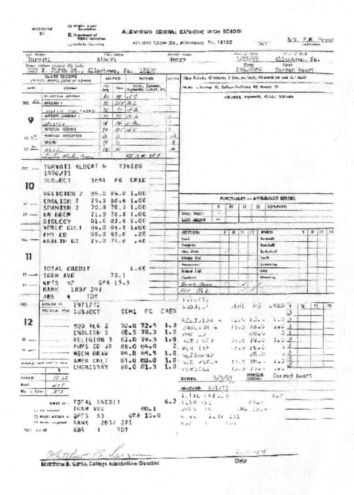

I am including my high school transcript as I wanted to inspire those that follow me. You can reverse negative findings and be successful.

On October 2023, we had our fiftieth high school reunion; it was the best one of all of the prior reunions.

Cliff and I

Pictured above I am with Cliff who was captain of our 1973 State Football Championship team. Cliff has organized every reunion since graduation; the fiftieth was the best. At the reunion, I had a classmate say, "I never thought you were very smart." I retorted surprise: I have two doctorates to your none—I win!

Prior to the reunion, I made an appointment with the principal and the ACCHS development department. I wanted to recreate a photo from my 1973 yearbook fifty years later.

1973   2023

After graduation, we had a short trip to the New Jersey shore. Shortly after that event, I left Allentown for the US Army.

Chapter 6

I received orders to report to the induction station in Wilkes Barre. The facility has since closed. The closure was attributed to the defense budget cuts and a 31 percent decline in military enlistments since 1989. The station had offered complete physical examinations, drug and alcohol tests, and medical consultations by local physicians at no cost to applicants from twenty-two counties. The station also operated seven mobile examining teams, which offered aptitude testing to applicants near their homes in Allentown, Hazleton, Lewisburg, North Towanda, Pottsville, Stroudsburg, and Williamsport. The station traces its history back to 1942, during the early stages of America's involvement in World War II.

Once we completed our physicals and assessment, we left the station by bus to Fort Dix,

New Jersey. Fort Dix was established in 1917 as Camp Dix, named for Major General John Adams Dix, who entered Army service as a fourteen-year-old cadet in the War of 1812 and mustered out as a captain in 1828; he later re-entered service as a major general in the Civil War.

Upon arrival, the cadre were super friendly welcoming us to the Army. We bunked down, and about 0500 the next morning, we were awakened by a screaming drill sergeant, I thought I died and went to hell. Thus, my eight weeks of basic training had started. We marched and marched and marched, learned weapons, chemical and biological, bivouac, first aid, and drill and ceremony—transforming a civilian into a soldier.

On a side note down the road from Fort Dix is the Deborah heart and Lung Center where in 1919 I started my heart surgery residency. Another linking of the Fates.

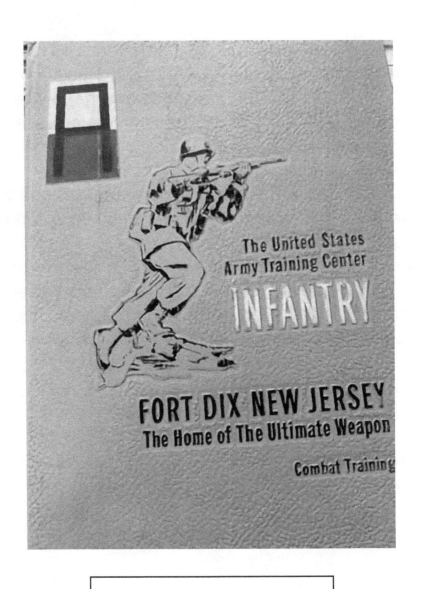

Fort Dix 1973 Yearbook

Basic Training photo

Basic weapon at the time was the M-16 A1 carbine.

Ammo was NATO 5.56×45mm. I qualified and was awarded a sharpshooter badge.

Once graduated from Basic Training, I was off to Fort Sam Houston, Texas, for basic 91 A Medic training. After eight weeks, I was ordered to Fort Jackson, South Carolina, to start my Clinical Specialists 91 C courser; this course was forty weeks in length. Once completed, I was ordered to Fort Belvoir, Virginia, for six months, and finally, ordered to Fort Monmouth, New Jersey. I was subsequently Honorably Discharged from the US Army.

Ranks Held

Private

Private First Class

Specialist
Fourth Class

Specialist Fifth
Class

Medals

National Defense Service Medal

Good Conduct Medal

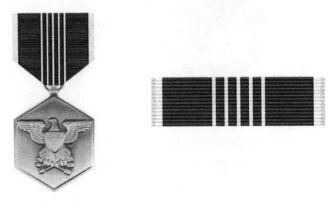

Army Commendation Medal

Sharpshooter Badge

Army Enlisted Medical Insignia

Chapter 7

After graduating from Cal State and entry into medical school, I was back in the Army as a commissioned officer US Army Reserves. The president of the United States at that time was Ronald Reagan.

I completed officers' course at Fort Sam Houston, Texas, during the summer of my first year of medical school.

This allowed me to do clinical rotations on a TDY (Temporary Duty Status) status and actually got paid. I did OB/Gyn, delivered 25 babies, 12 C-sections, and 14 tubal ligations in a four-week rotation. For an eight-week family medicine rotation, I was assigned to the Sixth Cavalry as a flight surgeon, did clinic in the morning, flew helicopters in the afternoon and evening, spent a week in south Texas along the Rio Grande, practicing for Middle East deployment.

I also completed air assault school.

Badges

Air Assault

Aeromedical Flight Badge

Medals

Cold War

★★★★★

Army Reserve Medal

Rank

Second Lieutenant

First Lieutenant

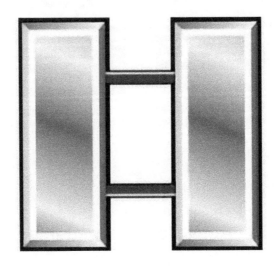

Captain

Major

42

Army Medical Corps Insignia

Putting it all together, my badges and ribbons

My time in the US Army was very fruitful. I learned that I indeed have leadership skills, had some outstanding medical training, as well as aviation medicine. The most important reward to me was not a medal or badge, but actually meeting my lovely WAC, Sharon. She changed my life as the Fates wove a golden thread into my tapestry of life.

Chapter 8

Cats

Sharon has always had a fondness for cats. I wrote in book 1 about the frozen cat she brought home to get warm. I was never allowed to have pets at home; my mom was afraid of animals. We decided she needed company, because I was going off to audition rotations out of state.

We adopted our first cat Atria from the North Texas Humane Society; she was a loving calico. Unfortunately, the kennel was infected with rhino syncytial virus—the majority of animals we euthanized. Sharon begged the vet to help her save her kitten; she would aspirate her airway so she could breathe, gave her breathing treatments, and she survived. She lived twenty-two years and passed away from a stroke.

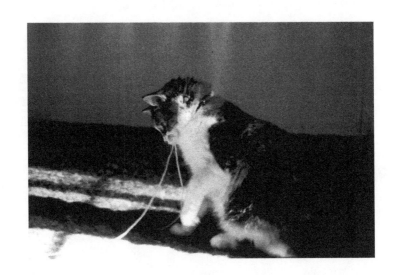

ATRIA

ATRIA

We decided to find a playmate for Atria, so we adopted our second cat *Systole*.

We obtained her from a breeder, who could not show her due to a kink in her tail. We got her for a reasonable price as Scottish Folds are rare and expensive.

The **Scottish Fold** is a distinctive breed of domestic cat characterized by a natural dominant gene mutation associated with <u>osteochondrodysplasia</u>. This genetic anomaly affects cartilage throughout the body, causing the ears to "fold," bending forward and down toward the front of the head. While this trait contributes to the breed's unique appearance, often described as owl-like, it has negative effects on the cat's welfare.

Originally called lop-eared or lops after the lop-eared rabbit, Scottish Fold became the breed's name in 1966. Depending on registries, longhaired Scottish Folds are varyingly known as Highland Fold, Scottish Fold Longhair, Longhair Fold and Coupari.

The original Scottish Fold was a white barn cat named Susie, who was found at a farm near Coupar Angus in Tayside, Scotland, in 1961. Susie's ears had an unusual fold in their middle, making her resemble an owl. When Susie had kittens, two of them were born with folded ears, and one was acquired by William Ross and his wife, Molly, neighboring farmers who were cat fanciers. The breeding program produced seventy-six kittens in the first three years—forty-two with folded ears and thirty-four with straight ears. The conclusion from this was that the ear mutation is due to a simple dominant gene.

Ross registered the breed with the Governing Council of the Cat Fancy (GCCF) in the United Kingdom in 1966 and started to breed Scottish Fold kittens with the help of geneticist Pat Turner. However by the early 1970s, the GCCF stopped registering the cat due to concerns about potential health issues such as ear infections and deafness. In 1970 the first Scottish Fold kittens were introduced to America via a Dr. Neil Todd of Massachusetts who was researching the mutation. Further cats were brought over, and the Scottish Fold breeding program continued with American Shorthairs and British Shorthairs being introduced.

In 1978 the Cat Fanciers' Association (CFA) granted the breed championship status. In the mid ninety eighties, the long-haired version started to gain recognition. The International Cat Association (TICA) was the first registry to recognized the longhairs for championship competition in the 1987–88 show season, and CFA followed in 1993–94.

Systole

She passed away at age twenty-three from kidney failure. We had a short hiatus of no kittens until we adopted the next set from a breeder in Arkansas "Purrfect Folds." So along come Tyre (straight ear) and Kira (folded ear) littermates.

Tyre

Kira

They both passed away at age twenty-one and twenty-two for kidney failure. Next up we adopted from the same breeder in Arkansas Skye and Terra Blue, both Scottish Folds—Skye, long hair; Terra Blue, short hair.

Skye

Terra Blue

Skye had a stroke at age eighteen. Terra Blue developed squamous cell carcinoma in her mouth; she was also eighteen. Then we adopted again from the North Tarrant Humane Society two strays—Diesel, our first male who was a talker due to Main Coon in him; and Heather, a sweet mixed breed. Diesel died of acute kidney failure at age eight; Heather is still alive as of this writing.

Diesel

Heather

So we are not done. At one time we had six cats, four cat boxes, and a lot of food. I count going into the veterinarian bills, as they are cared for by a wonderful feline vet in Southlake, Dr K., at Kitten to Cat Hospital.

Next up is Bella who is now three years old as of this writing; we found her from a local breeder. We got ripped off with an online breeder that cost me $4,000 and no cat! The breeder in our area was wonderful and very caring of their kittens. She is doing well and is sweet; she gets along with our newest kittens.

Bella

Finally, we have the newest additions, a set of twin Scottish Folds, Heid and Hannah. They are now two years old as of this writing and are a joy to see them play. They also are somewhat snuggly, and as usual, they like to be nearby people.

Hannah and Heidi

Now you know our "clan." They give Sharon some company while I am at the university or away on conference or book signings. This group will be our last; we already have provisions in our wills for them to be cared for in the lap of luxury.

Chapter 9

Fiftieth Anniversary

It's hard to believe fifty years together. We met in 1973, married in 1974, and here we are in 2024, fifty years later. It has been reported that 33 percent of surgeons are divorced. There are many factors to include: burnout, duty hours, loss of intimacy, financial strains. We were fortunate in that we continued to work as a team. We kept laughter, love, and passion in the marriage.

1974

1989 5th Anniversary

1994 40th Anniversary

45th Anniversary

50ʰ Anniversary

Military Ordinariate
United States of America
1011 FIRST AVENUE
NEW YORK, N.Y. 10022
✠

Certificate of Marriage

ALBERT HENRY YURVATI

and ...... SHARON ANN CURRY ... (DONELAN) ......

were lawfully married on the ....31....... day of ....August....., ...1974

according to the Rite of the Catholic Church

at ...Patriot, Ft. Lee, Virginia......, Reverend ....Thomas David Welch..

officiating, in the presence of ......Thomas Johns......

and ......Deborah Govemski...... witnesses.

Date ..December 18, 1974

Record No..281827......

....J. F. Marhach....
Signature

Sharon had to get permission from her commander, and the Department of the Army cut orders for us to marry. At the time, female active duty soldiers, once married, could be released from their commitments. Sharon stayed until I completed my three years.

COMMONWEALTH OF VIRGINIA
STATE DEPARTMENT OF HEALTH, RICHMOND

CERTIFICATE OF MARRIAGE

I CERTIFY THAT ON THIS DATE AT Patriots Chapel, Fort Lee,...... VIRGINIA, BY

AUTHORITY OF A LICENSE ISSUED BY THE CLERK OF THE...District......COURT

OF ......Hopewell...... CITY OR COUNTY, STATE OF VIRGINIA, DATED THE

31st DAY OF...August......, 19..76.., I JOINED TOGETHER IN MARRIAGE:

Albert Henry Yurvati......, HUSBAND, AND...Sharon Ann Curry (Donelan), HIS WIFE.

GIVEN UNDER MY HAND THIS...31st....DAY OF......August......, 19..74..

Thomas David Welch
(SIGNATURE OF OFFICIANT)

Chaplain (CPT) USA
Catholic Chaplain
(TITLE OF OFFICIANT)

50 Years

600 Months
2608.93 Weeks
18262.5 Days
26,270,000 Minute
1,577,836,800 Seconds

AND COUNTING

Yes! It's quite a milestone. We continue to be together despite the Fates' interference with our health. Good news is the gold thread is still strong that binds, that even the Fates can't undo.

Chapter 10

Doctorates

Based on my prior academics in high school, I never would have perceived that in my lifetime, I would hold three doctorates. According to available data, the percentage of the population with multiple doctorates is extremely small, generally considered to be less than 1 percent of the population; meaning only a very tiny fraction of people hold more than one doctoral degree.

Even having a single doctorate is relatively rare, with only a small percentage of the population achieving that level of education.

Individuals with multiple doctorates are often found in highly specialized fields where extensive research across different disciplines is required.

Precise statistics on the exact percentage of people with multiple doctorates might be difficult to find due to the small number of individuals involved.

So in ,essence I am now a Doctor, Doctor, Doctor, or a Doctor[3].

My first doctorate, DO, from TCOM, 1986.

My second doctorate, a PhD, from Northcentral University, 2015.

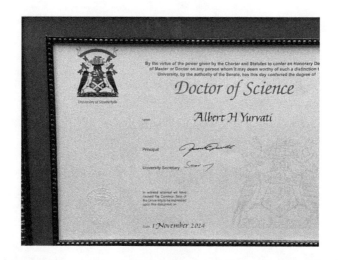

By the virtue of the power given by the Charter and Statutes to confer an Honorary De
of Master or Doctor on any person whom it may deem worthy of such a distinction t
University, by the authority of the Senate, has this day conferred the degree of

Doctor of Science

Albert H Yurvati

Principal

University Secretary

In witness whereof we have
caused the Common Seal of
the University to be impressed
upon this document on

1 November 2024

My third doctorate from the University of Strathclyde, Glasgow, Scotland. This is a very special degree; prior recipients include Nelson Mandela, King Olaf of Norway, multiple Nobel Laureates and CEOs.

Universities in Scotland do a ceremonial "capping" when they bestow a degree. It's still hard to believe as I was told "You are not very smart." Well, I guess I proved them wrong!

Chapter 11

Book Signing

Participated in a few book fairs doing book signing and interviews.

My first was the London Book Fair.

It was very successful—met many interesting people.

Next was the Los Angeles Times Book Festival.

Next was the Miami Book Fair on November 2024. All have been very successful venues; we ran out of books by the second day.

Chapter 12

Patient Safety

As a provider, you see one side of patient safety, but as a patient, you experience defects in patient safety. There have been multiple errors that could have cost me my life. Luckily as a professional, I could identify and intervene on behalf of myself.

UNTHSC TCOM embarked on a patient safety mission, directed by Dr. Lillie and her contacts with the Institute of Healthcare Improvement (IHI). We allocated two weeks out of the six-week surgery rotation for a comprehensive patient safety segment that ultimately led to an international certification, CPPS (Certified Professional in Patent Safety). The program started on July 2020, and as of November 9, 2024, we have had 1,000 students certified. We are the only medical school that the IHI has allowed certification of medical students. Our passing rate is about 97 percent versus the

IHI passing rate of 74 percent. Out of all certified by the IHI, there are about 7,000 certified by the Certification Board for Healthcare Improvement (CBPPS). With certification, TCOM graduates are well prepared to meet the Accreditation Council for Graduate Medical Education (ACGME) Patient Safety and Quality Improvement milestones. The Milestones are competency-based developmental outcomes (e.g., knowledge, skills, attitudes, and performance) that can be demonstrated progressively by residents/fellows from the beginning of their education through graduation to the unsupervised practice of their specialties. Residents are assessed twice a year based on the milestones.

The TCOM Patient Safety Course addresses the milestones related to the Systems-Based Practice Core Competency: Patient Safety and Quality Improvement. In their first year of residency, TCOM graduates are demonstrating high levels of performance.

Currently, we are studying the results of our students as PGY1 residents and their rating on ACGME Milestones as relating to patient safety. Preliminary review appears very significant; our former students are being rated on a 5-point scale 3–5. This is very significant, and we are hopeful they will make a positive impact on patient safety.

Epilogue

This book concludes my series. The title comes from our trainer Dr. LBM; we had to recite specifically to the perfusionist: *"2.2, 30 degrees, on bypass."*

I hope you have enjoyed the series; we are maintaining, hoping that the multiple myeloma remains quiescent. I am contemplating writing a totally different book: *Bride and Blades: How to Survive a Surgical Marriage*. It will be a guide for students, residents, and new attending surgeons. Also, in the works is the book *American College of Osteopathic Surgeons 100-Year Legacy*. I am a co-editor with two colleagues. The last book was published in 1995 by Doctor Ellis Siefer, *The American College of Osteopathic Surgeons: A Proud History*.